The Wildebeest and a Bunch of Crock
and Other Animal Story Poems

Praise for this book:

"*The Wildebeest and a Bunch of Crock and Other Animal Story Poems* by Jeffry Glover is a collection of light-hearted and humorous poems that educate and delight children and adults alike .... easy to read, rhythmical, entertaining, ... creative, playful, and clever."

—Jennie More for Readers' Favorite

Also by Jeffry Glover:

"*9 Lively Cat Tales and Other Pet Poems* is quite simply pure fun.... delightfully purrfect!...Any pet owner or animal lover will enjoy this lively and often humorous look at the world according to cats (and dogs)."

—Emily-Jane Hills Orford for Readers' Favorite

"What an impressive collection of varied tributes to our furry friends, filled with frisky wit and whimsy, sure to delight animal lovers of all ages."

—Sylvia Kremp, Language Arts Teacher and Librarian

To find more books by Jeffry Glover,
please visit www.PoemsforPleasurePress.com

The Wildebeest and a Bunch of Crock
and Other Animal Story Poems

Jeffry Glover

POEMS FOR PLEASURE PRESS
Stoughton, Wisconsin

Copyright 2023 Jeffry Glover. All rights reserved. No part of this work may be reproduced, transmitted, or distributed by any means, electronic or mechanical, without express written permission of the author except for brief excerpts, which may be quoted in reviews. For permission to use material from this book please contact the publisher.

Published by Poems for Pleasure Press LLC
contact@poemsforpleasurepress.com
Stoughton, Wisconsin, United States of America
Order books online at www.PoemsforPleasurePress.com

Publisher's Cataloging-in-Publication
(Provided by Cassidy Cataloguing Services, Inc.)

Names:	Glover, Jeffry (Jeffry Keith), 1946- author. | Bausman, Mary, designer.
Title:	The wildebeest and a bunch of crock, and other animal story poems / Jeffry Glover ; [cover by Mary Bausman].
Description:	First edition. | Stoughton, Wisconsin : Poems for Pleasure Press, 2023. | Interest age level: 12 and up.
Identifiers:	ISBN: 978-1948854047 (hardcover) | 978-1948854054 (softcover) | 978-1948854061 (ebook-ePub) | LCCN: 2023911323
Subjects:	LCSH: Animals--Poetry. | Nature--Poetry. | LCGFT: Animal poetry. | Humorous poetry. | Stories in rhyme. | BISAC: HUMOR / Topic / Animals. | HUMOR / Form / Limericks & Verse. | POETRY / Subjects & Themes / Nature. | NATURE / Animals / Wildlife.
Classification:	LCC: PS3607.L6844 W55 2023 | DDC: 811/.6--dc23
	Library of Congress Control Number: 2023911323

The author gratefully acknowledges the cover design by Mary Bausman, interior design by KJ Forest, and PCIP by Cassidy Cataloguing Services. The author draws inspiration from many sources, including Sara Rath's excellent *About Cows* (Northwood Press: Minocqua, 1987) for the poem "Cows in Space." Fonts: ©2010 The Crimson Text Project Authors (github.com/googlefonts/Crimson), ©2018 The Crimson Pro Project Authors (github.com/Fonthausen/CrimsonPro), and ©2016 The Nunito Sans Project Authors (github.com/Fonthausen/NunitoSans), licensed under the SIL Open Font License, Version 1.1 viewable at https://scripts.sil.org/OFL. Author photo by Express Portraits.

To support sustainability Poems for Pleasure Press books are printed on archival quality, responsibly sourced paper by Lightning Source according to sustainability practices per www.ingramspark.com/environmental-responsibility.

First Edition 2023
Printed in the United States of America

Contents

Introduction 1
I. Animal Fables 3
   The Wildebeest and a Bunch of Crock 4
   Cows In Space 8
   Mister Twister and His Sister 11
   Cricket in a Thicket 14
   The Porcupine 16
   Gnu Unanswered Questions 18
   The Swan, the Duck, and the Ring 22
II. Tall Tales 25
   Baboon Won't Use a Spoon 26
   Never Knew a Gnu 27
   A Questionable Interview 27
   Elevator Alligator 28
   The Sloth 30
   Giraffic Park 31
   The Old Gnu 32
   Four Bear 34
   A Thoroughbred's Racy Remarks 35
   Cow Dreams 36

Polar Bear's Complaints 37
III. Animals Got Talent 39
   Bears Jazzin' 40
   Elk and Welk 42
   Almost Famous 43
   After You 43
   Giraffe Basketball 44
   Winning Attitude 45
   To Answer a Call 45
   Birds Playing Musical Chairs 46
   One Small Condition 47
   Piano Bird 48
IV. Small Tales 51
   Papa Possum 52
   Wash for Dinner 53
   Garter Snake Etiquette 53
   Who You Resemble 54
   Mouse Repast 56
   The Gray Squirrel 59
   The Skunk 60
   The Beetle and the Horseshoe 62
   The Hedgehog 64
V. Four-legged Tales 65
   Fox with Moxie 66

One Sly Fox 67
Acacia Devotee 67
Elephant Walk 68
A Bear and Bees 72
The Graceful Giraffe 73
A Simple Life 74
The Savanna Elephant 75
The White-tailed Deer 76
VI. To Sea What We Can See 77
The Starfish 78
The Seahorse 79
Piranha Lunch 80
No Boat for Crocodile Throat 82
Blue Marlins 83
Wonders of the Octopus 84
Meditation on Returning Salmon 85
Catch a Bite to Eat 85
VII. Feathered Tales 87
Peacock Eyes 88
Penguin Parade 89
The Bird Nest 90
Owl Scowl 91
A Vee of Geese 92
Feeding Cranes 93

Turkey Survival 94
Royal Peacocks 95
Four Foolish Crows 96
VIII. What's in a Name? 99
A Gnu Spelling 100
The Zonkey 101
The Peliphant 102
The Leopon 104
Mongooses 105
Defamed Misnamed Animals 106
The X-itee 108
The Frumious Bandersnatch 109
The Unicorn You May See 110
What Birds Are 111
About the Author 113

Introduction

Dear Reader:

The animal world has long captured my imagination, which I find flows through my pen onto the written page. I've collected many wildlife stories, told in rhyming verse, and wish to invite you along on a tour of my menagerie. The animals featured here range from the well-known to the very unusual to the occasionally highly speculative creatures we may come across in our life travels. On this adventure you will discover dozens of wild animal tales that are fun to read aloud and share with family and friends. In the pages of this book you'll meet a wildebeest that a crafty crocodile is trying to entice to take a swim, courageous cows-moo-nauts rocketing to the moon, a joyful band of jazz-playing bears, a zonkey, and a peliphant, all in playful poems presented here for your entertainment. Turn the page for the tour to begin!

Jeffry Glover

I. Animal Fables

The Wildebeest and a Bunch of Crock

On the high muddy banks of the river Zambezi
Stood a brave wildebeest; he was feeling uneasy
Since he wanted to cross where the river was wide,
But he feared muddy waters where danger could hide.

In the water below lay a fierce crocodile.
Cunning, his teeth betrayed a sly smile.
The game that he played we could call hide-and-seek,
Which he learned as a youth in his home, Mozambique.

Now the truth is this croc was impatient to eat,
Clever, however, and hid his deceit,
For he knew if he waited for a fat wildebeest
To cross the Zambezi he'd have a great feast.

'Twould be, he believed, just a matter of time
Till down to the riverbank a wildebeest must climb
And dash fast past predators, of which he was one,
Awaiting a moment of delicious fun.

Ferocious, atrocious, with his friends cheek-to-cheek,
This croc smacked his chops there in hot Mozambique.
He whetted his whistle, excited to wait
Until that poor wildebeest tempted cruel fate.

Now the wildebeest wasn't as dumb as you'd think.
He'd seen friends before him dash into the drink,
Never again to be seen...in one piece.
He was wise to this game of famine or feast.

He knew about danger in this, the Zambezi.
His instincts were saying, "A monster could seize me.
Et tu brute?" he recalled from veldt grammar school
And from roaming near lions; this 'beest was no fool.

He'd heard of sharp daggers attached to a jaw,
Read his Coke and his Blackstone; he knew jungle law.
Hence courting great danger near a fearful reptile
Gave him pause most especially if it be crocodile.

So now there he stood looking down at the river,
Wanting to jump, but his gut was aquiver.
What should he do? Should he leap? Take a chance?
He waited and pondered, his thoughts all askance.

"Quit stalling. Just jump!" roared a croc from below.
"One, two, three, four, five, six—get ready, set, go!
My friends all are waiting; we don't have all day.
Leap now or move over! Let other 'beests play."

"I'm thinking! I'm thinking! Be patient, will you?"
Cried the wary wildebeest. "That's the least you can do.
I will not be rushed by some voice in the water.
I refuse to be rushed, to risk life, limb, or slaughter."

This said, all the crocs down below gave a groan.
Their stomachs were growling; they all made a moan.
"Look here, wildebeest, just for you such a deal
We'll make if you hurry. We want you to feel

"No jumper's remorse, not the least hesitation,
Complete satisfaction. It'll be like vacation.
Imagine you're diving into a warm pool
At a luxury resort, or you're on a bar stool

"Quaffing a drink, tipsy, ready to fall,
But first want a swim on your way to the mall,
A quick little swim, maybe you and a friend.
Life's short, after all, that's what I'd recommend."

The wildebeest was tempted; it sounded quite good
And yet he was puzzled. Had he understood
This recommendation for a little vacation?
Was it real or a crock of reptilian imagination?

And what had occasioned it? What was the reason,
This deal being proffered during migrating season?
He wasn't too sure. It just didn't ring right.
His concern seemed to grow. He was feeling uptight.

"I'm waiting! Hurry up!" growled the croc once again.
"Your time's running out. Hurry up if you can.
Just do it, get through it, don't worry about a thing.
Action's what counts. Action gives your life zing."

The wildebeest laughed, "He must think me a fool.
I know crocs are liars; I've been to law school
So I'm fully aware no croc can be trusted,
But with a little deceit they just might get busted."

"Oh croc," called the wildebeest, "About that vacation
You promise—sounds great in my imagination—
It's brilliant. It's bully. I love it, I do.
It's so marvelous and tempting. Let's make it come true.

"But before my vacation I first need your aid
To help me fulfill a commitment I've made.
Down yonder round the bend on the river Zambezi
I need help herding hippos, but it ought to be easy.

"Where they are swimming and taking their ease—
Where mamas are guarding their precious babies—
Is a place that's off limits; they shouldn't be there.
Please help them get moved; I don't care to where.

"Just find them and tell them and push them to go.
Chase them if need be. Say you want them to know
They just cannot stay there, they must move away
Not tomorrow or next week, but right now, today.

Say, 'Move it, you mamas. Get out of this river.
Take your babies, vamoose! You simply can't live here.'
And if they resist here's what you must do:
Push them and shove them till their moving is through,

"And when you've done this, come back and I'll cross
This river Zambezi. I'll do it because
You've done me this favor and I'll owe you one.
Now go herd those hippos—have serious fun!

"Take all of your relatives and take every friend,
Every crocodile here, take them all 'round the bend.
And while you are there, I'll stand here and guard
Your place in the river. It won't be that hard."

And with the deal made, all the crocs swam away
Following his directions, yet to this very day
Not one has returned. So the wildebeests crossed
The river Zambezi without a single soul lost.

What happened to the crocodiles they never did know.
One never can tell with a croc and hippo.
Some think hippos love to break crocodile backs.
Some claim they engage in crocodile attacks.

Some say crocs don't get on too well with those beasts.
Some say of those crocs every one is deceased.
The wildebeests aren't concerned crossing river or creek,
Not lately at least if they're from Mozambique.

Cows In Space

"Spaced Out Cows: NASA sent some cows up in space in a rocket a few years ago, to orbit the earth and test their reactions to outer space. It was the herd shot round the world."
— Sara Rath in *About Cows* (Northwords Press: Minoqua, 1987)

The news has moos in it today
The rocketeers at NASA say,
News that cows were shot to space,
No longer just the human race.

They've gone up there, so papers tell,
As cows-moo-nauts and doing well
Orbiting around the earth,
Mooing and chewing cud with mirth,

Happily content to go
Around our planet, while below
Admiring farmers there will cheer
Since cows have pierced the stratosphere.

This deed is splendid, such a feat
Of dairy-do, hard to beat—
Remarkable that cows fly faster
High above their grassy pasture.

Far below they see their barn,
But cows-moo-nauts don't give a darn
Since now they're famous—why should they,
Floating weightless, munching hay?

Cape Cownaveral cleared them to go,
To the moon for this will show
Cows in space aren't temporary,
Not some fad of do-or-dairy.

Rather, it's their chance to be
The first bovines in history
To reach the moon all shiny bright
Glowing in the dark of night.

But first they need to make it there,
Cow-operate, and take great care
Because the moon is far away,
Though getting closer every day.

They're heroes and deserve to be;
It behooves them to make history,
To land four hooves upon the ground,
Take cow steps and trot around,

Sing *Moon River*, plant a flag,
Ring their cow bells loudly, brag,
Take some samples of moon dirt,
Do such things, it wouldn't hurt.

Finally, they rocket near,
Over the radio they hear a cheer:
"Cows, you're cleared to go on down,
Touch the ground, and look around."

And so they land, but not on grass,
Only moondust, wide and vast.
They're on the ladder, set to bound—
Just one last rung to reach the ground.

"That's one small step, one big wow,
One giant leap for a Jersey cow!"
This is history, nothing less.
Celebrate! Inform the press!

Cowabunga! This is great!
They made it happen—mark the date!
This is udderly incredible,
Though moondust is hardly edible,

Not like clover sweet to eat.
Never mind, it's quite a feat
Just to reach the moon and land.
Give these 'nauts a hoof (er, hand)!

    * Postscript *

All the cowsmoonauts returned
To tell tall tales of what they learned,
Like the moon is made of cheddar cheese
Except for craters filled with bries.

Those brave cows leave us with these thoughts:
That heifers can be cows-moo-nauts,
And do such deeds with all due speed
Proving that they can succeed.

There's something new under the sun
That cows in space have just begun.
Will they next jump over the moon, past Mars,
And fly through space to reach the stars?

Mister Twister and His Sister

Mama Cow said to her son,
"Mister Twister, since you've done
All your chores, take Nell, your sister,
To the County Fair for fun."

So Mister Twister and his sister
Dressed for the County Fair.
Before they left his sister asked,
"How do you like my hair?"

Mister Twister took a look.
"Turn around, let's see.
Front looks fine, but there in back
It seems too flat to me."

"Mercy me! Oh, that won't do.
My hairdo just won't do!"
Said Mister Twister's little sister,
"But wait! I'm not yet through."

Nell left her stall to fix her hair.
Her brother took a chair
And while he waited patiently
His mind daydreamed somewhere.

Back came sister with a smile.
She'd frizzied up her hair.
"Ready? Let's go," her brother said,
And got up from his chair.

"I think my hair is better now.
How do you like my dress?"
"Good...I guess...though I have doubts...."
"Doubts about my dress?"

"It's the color—light chartreuse—
That's quite hard to ignore."
His sister frowned, turned around,
And closed the barnyard door.

She hurried past the hayloft then
To see what could be found.
Her brother took his chair again,
And chewed his cud around.

In a quarter hour (or slightly more),
Nell, wearing a different dress,
Checked her reflection with a grin
And asked brother to assess.

"How's this, better than before?
Sometimes it's hard to choose."
"Oh, yes," said Mister Twister,
"But what about those shoes!"

"What's wrong with them? I thought they went
With what I'm wearing now.
I bought them last year for the fair.
Expensive—holy cow!"

"I'm sorry, Nell, but to be frank,
Those shoes are showing wear.
The fit is fair, but look down there,
You see that little tear?"

She turned around, her face a-frown,
Be-frazzled in this case.
She couldn't wear them to the fair
And risk a shoe disgrace.

"I've just the thing, the shoes to bring;
I'm sure they'll look quite fine.
I'll be right back, they're near my stall,
I'll give them a quick shine."

She went back to her stanchion and
Strolled past the creaky door,
Tossed the torn shoes she had on
And changed her shoes once more.

Then called, "I'm ready, Mister Twister,
To hoof it to the fair
In my muumuu with matching shoes
That I picked out with care."

Mister Twister, looking nervous,
Paced around the floor.
Nell asked once more, "How do I look?"
While waltzing through the door.

"Cowabunga! Cowabunga!
Your muumuu is so bright,
But it does go with those shoes—
A truly splendid sight!"

They had such fun when they arrived,
Then to their great surprise
The judges at the fair approved:
For style Nell won first prize!

Cricket in a Thicket

Crawling through a thicket,
Ant heard a cricket sigh,
"Life's a sticky wicket,"
To which ant made reply:

"Cheer up, chirping friend;
That's my best advice.
Life is rarely easy,
Sometimes not so nice.

"But wickets can be mastered,
Or endured at least,
By the large and mighty,
Down to the smallest beast.

"Strive to build your life,
Work for what you yearn,
Educate yourself
And learn! Learn! Learn!

"Make your dreams come true
With every step you take,
Steady as you go
With so much at stake.

"Give it all you've got!
In your own self trust,
Live every day with joy,
Have courage and be just."

Across the thicket cricket
Chirped that he had heard
This, the ant's advice,
Every single word.

Since then he chirps each day,
And loves his work and play.
He's feeling, well, quite "cricket,"
And goes his merry way.

The Porcupine

How tranquil is the porcupine.
If undisturbed he's quite benign,
But do take note of his design
Especially if you be canine.

I say to those who might incline
To bother him and intertwine:
Do not approach his scrimmage line
Unless you are prepared to whine.

For if you choose to needle him
Upon a curious foolish whim,
The trouble you'll be getting in
Has one prognosis and it's grim.

I knew a dog who tried one day
Approach a porcupine to play
With no forethought for his foray
And how it might bring him dismay.

When in fact the pup jumped in,
'Twas like a cushion to a pin,
And sooner than one might suppose
He met with woes all 'round his nose,

Which goes to show one ought to go
With unfamiliar critters slow,
Not rush in fast, and as a rule
Don't get too close, for looks can fool.

The pup, poor thing, I'm sure he felt
Each painful prick, each swollen welt
Upon his nose, forepaws and pelt—
Big TROUBLE was the word they spelt—

While porcupine went on its way
None the worse for doggie play,
Just like any other day
When canine capers do not pay.

Gnu Unanswered Questions*

What does the gnu do in the zoo?
Have you ever wondered or wished you knew?

What kind of recreation does he pursue?
Does he play all day or work hard too?

Some answer yes, but I leave it to you
To tell me what a gnu does do.

Does he go in public or use the loo?
Does he gobble grass or does he chew?

Are his habits old or mostly new?
Is he patient waiting in a queue?

Who does he see when he feels blue
Or when he's sick and has the flu?

When he wants a stylish new 'do,
Does he use Brill Cream or some other goo?

When he's in the shower, does he use shampoo?
At the barbershop is his haircut crew?

When he meets you, does he say, "Howdy-do"
Or "Look out, baby. I'm coming through"?

Is he a strict vegetarian or does he eat stew?
Does he like Swiss cheese or only bleu?

Is he a serious reader of Camus,
Or does he prefer Winnie the Pooh?

Has he watched cartoons about Mister Magoo,
Or if not, how about Scooby-doo?

What newspapers will he most peruse
And subscriptions can he not refuse?

Is his favorite color bright chartreuse
Or does he prefer cool hues like blues?

Are his interests broad or are they few?
Can he blow his horn when he wants to?

Does he wear old clothes or usually new?
Does he keep them pressed or all askew?

Does he drink cream soda or tea-for-two,
Cappuccino or some other brew?

When he eats, does he have enough for two?
Does he like beer brats at a barbecue?

If he dined with pandas, would he eat bamboo,
Or stick to his favorite, cordon bleu?

Is charitable fundraising what he likes to do,
And if so, how much would he ask from you?

At football games, does he ever boo?
Would the team he roots for be Purdue?

When he acts on stage, does he miss his cue
Or go on after some other small snafu?

Is he in a band and play kazoo
Or participate in a musical revue?

When he hums is it usually "Doo-be-doo"?
What bad habits does he most eschew?

When he goes to church and sits in a pew
Does he sing and shout out "Hallelu"?

Will he cheer at a rodeo like a buck-a-roo?
If he makes a promise, will he keep it, too?

Has he studied karate and kung fu?
Has he also taken jujitsu?

Was he in the navy? Does he have a tattoo?
Is it mostly hidden or in plain view?

Has he cruised overseas on the QEII?
Did he volunteer to be part of the crew?

Has he traveled by car, but wished he flew,
Or waited for a bus standing in a queue?

Has he taken a vacation to Honolulu
And worn a muumuu on Oahu?

Can he give a speech impromptu?
Has he ever experienced déjà vu?

Is his very best friend a kangaroo
Or another critter at the zoo?

When he wants to court and starts to woo,
Will he tend to grunt or will he moo?

Is he a gentleman dating through and through?
Approaching a door, does he say, "After you"?

Does he wonder what this world's coming to?
Does he ever worry he'll end up glue?

Does he think someday he'll say adieu
And wonder where his whole life flew?

What is life like for a gnu?
Gnus may know, but how about you?

---
*A gnu is another name for a wildebeest.

The Swan, the Duck, and the Ring

Ages ago in days long gone,
There lived a mallard and his friend, a swan,
Who would dilly-dally, swim, and duck
For food found buried in pond muck

Searching for snacks they could pluck,
Like minnows and such caught by luck
While living bird lives of the leisure class,
Ducking bills downward while up went their … rear.

That's what they did season after season
Seizing the day for no particular reason.
Till it happened by chance one early spring
The duck while out ducking spied a ruby ring.

"Look what I've found!" cried the happy duck.
"I'm going to be rich!" (He was thunderstruck.)
"Beginner's luck, duck," declared the swan.
"Mark my words, friend—easy got, easy gone."

"What do you mean?" the surprised duck replied,
To which swan smiled and off did glide.
"What can swan know that I do not?"
Mused the duck as he thought and thought,

And pondered what he should do with the ring:
Keep it or sell it? What price would it bring?
What was the ring worth and who might pay
For a ring like this one anyway?

Just then in the sky an eagle flew by
Searching for prey (always worth a try),
When suddenly he spied the duck down below.
What was duck holding he wanted to know.

Circling, he saw something shiny and red
On the wing of the duck and so down he sped.
"Duck, what have you there, may I inquire?"
The eagle asked. "It looks bright as fire."

"Fire? Not this!" quacked the duck. "It's a ring
That a pretty price at an auction will bring."
"How much is it worth?" asked the Eagle. "Tell me more:
The price of your life or would you rather be poor?"

At this the duck quaked, he shivered and shook
Thinking over the question. (Half a second it took.)
"Mister Eagle," he said. "It's worth way more than that,
But for you there's no charge, Quack! Quack! Quack!"

"Deal!" screeched the eagle. "Mine and I'm gone.
Got one last year just like that from the swan."
Off with the ring flew the eagle to soar,
Bad luck for the duck who was rich no more.

"Better to be poor than rich and dead.
Living's the thing," the wise swan said.
"What's easily got is easily gone.
Don't give it another thought – just move on.

"Anyway, who needs a ruby ring?
Your life's worth more than that old thing."
There's a lesson here: Riches are fine,
But if the price is too high, duck them, decline.

II. Tall Tales

Baboon Won't Use a Spoon

The bold baboon won't use a spoon
When he consumes his lunch at noon,
Won't even use it as a scoop
When he wants to gulp his soup,
No, a spoon he cannot master,
So eating soup equals disaster.
Nor will he drink it with a straw;
He'd rather dip, then suck his paw.
Just pulls the bowl up to his face
And slurps it down, a real disgrace!
Oh, who knows what this baboon's thinking
When he lifts his bowl for drinking?
And the way he'll crush each cracker
Into crumbs just causes laughter.
Compared to how some baboons eat,
Other creatures look quite neat.
So if you give his bowl a fill
You can be sure his soup will spill.
Just know he's hopeless with a spoon,
At breakfast, dinner, or at noon.
He's known to toss his bowl, not wash it
In the sink under a faucet;
Just stares, then blinks and leaves the room,
And most agree it's none too soon.
At etiquette he's no success;
No matter what, he'll make a mess.
Though he may try, he can't compete
At manners when there's soup to eat.

Never Knew a Gnu

I never knew a gnu, did you?
Nor very well a lion,
But I can tell you of the two
Which one to keep an eye on.

A Questionable Interview

We asked a lion and then a gnu
If they would do an interview.
At our suggestion we'd ask a question,
Maybe even two.
"I won't decline," said the lion.
"I'll do it, too," replied the gnu.
"When shall we meet?" the lion asked.
"Soon," said the gnu," Let's make it fast."
But when they met, one was et.
I think it was the gnu.
So much for lions, and gnus tryin'
To meet for an interview.

Elevator Alligator

Once I met an alligator
In a hotel elevator
Heading for the 50th floor,
Or maybe it was 54.

Seemed to be on staff, a waiter,
Or a room service alligator.
Didn't say a word to me,
Just carried a dinner tray, you see.

Didn't turn to left or right,
Yet I was terrified as might
Be anyone who has to ride
An elevator with a gator inside.

Shocked I was, yes, in a fright,
Fearing the gator really might
I don't know exactly what,
Eat me there or something, but

What's a gator going to do
Who is professional through and through?
So up I rode with this reptile.
He didn't move all the while,

Didn't say a single word.
If he had, I would have heard.
When finally we reached 54,
Suddenly the elevator door

Opened and he slithered out
On his way, I had no doubt,
To deliver someone's scrumptious food,
Which I admit smelled pretty good,

Like a steak with baked potater,
Thanks to that helpful gator waiter.
He disappeared and I went on,
Glad to have the gator gone.

Good help is hard to find these days,
But hotels have their hiring ways
Apparently, and sooner or later,
Some may hire an alligator.

The Everglades are full of them,
So if they're short of help is when
Recruiters go and find a few;
The better hotels will train them, too,

To do whatever work they've got,
Deliver food, drinks, and whatnot,
Give swimming lessons, serve as cooks,
Or catch fresh fish from local brooks,

Bake 'em, broil 'em, even fry.
Really, folks, this ain't no lie.
So the next time you ride in an elevator,
Don't be surprised if it's with a gator!

The Sloth

Slow and steady goes the sloth
Moving through the trees,
Doesn't hurry, doesn't worry;
He is at his ease.
Nothing seems to matter much
Judging from his face.
Let other creatures run about;
He has his own slow pace.
Haste is not his habit, no;
He's always slow and steady,
Storing up his energy,
Ready to be ready
To move on, to be gone,
Or to a mate beguile.
Going fast is not his way,
Speed is not his style.
Ask him when he'll do his chores,
He will only smile
And answer you indefinite:
"Oh ... maybe... in ... a ... while."

Giraffic Park

Giraffic Park is a neck of land
Planned as a zoo, we understand,
Where gentle giants can stand tall
And live apart from others small.
With four big legs, long and strong,
Giraffes can roam and get along,
Eating leaves on acacia trees,
Reaching them with browsing ease,
Separated from each thorn
At breakfast time every morn,
Stretching to a heady height,
Tranquil in the morning light
With not one dinosaur in sight
Except for all the birds in flight.*

---
*It's thought that birds evolved from dinosaurs.

The Old Gnu

The gnu was old, no longer bold,
A lioness could see.
He couldn't run for fright or fun,
For far too slow was he.

One day he heard his herd would move
To find far greener grass.
The question was would a lioness
Give chase or let him pass.

With fear untold his blood ran cold
To such a great degree,
He nearly froze, not self-controlled,
Like you or I might be.

The lioness soon picked him out
To be an easy kill,
And followed him all round about
With sneaky sleuthing skill.

The herd could sense the lion there
And they began to run.
The lioness was well aware
The battle could be won

Before she even made a charge,
And followed on gnu's tail.
Success she thought was written large,
Quite sure she couldn't fail.

With strength and speed she would succeed—
That confident was she—
To bring the gnu down soon and feed!
How easy it would be.

The race was on, the gnu began
To run as best he could,
The lion gaining on him ran,
Its chances looking good.

Across the veldt with strength of will
The two cut to the chase,
And yet the gnu ahead was still;
He kept a steady pace.

The gnu's hard hoofs kicked up much dust
That flew into the eyes
Of the lioness there just
Before she had her prize.

"Take that!" the gnu laughed
With a snort, "I may yet win this race."
The lion growled; she could not grasp
The gnu, dust in her face.

Then in dismay and in a daze
The lioness was done,
All tuckered out, she slowed her pace;
The gnu had actually won.

Although no longer in his prime
Life's lessons he could trust;
Old gnu had beat the odds this time
With luck and pluck and dust.

Four Bear

Bears in a cave lay sound asleep
Snoozing after counting sheep,

When one awoke, all gruff, and said,
"My stomach's bare—I must be fed.

I'm hungry, famished, in the mood
For berry pie, my favorite food."

The second bear growled when he heard
The berry word, and then the third.

The last bear slept well, unaware,
Except to snore, "Forbear! Forbear!"

A Thoroughbred's Racy Remarks

There was a horse, a thoroughbred,
Who said, "The way to get ahead
Is run like hell when you hear the bell;
That way you may do well."
"The race," he said, "Goes to the strong.
Am I right or am I wrong?
You can't be late at the gate;
There's too much there at stake.
You want to win, that's how it's been,
And so you always must begin
At a pace to win your race;
Each steed must speed with grace.
And now," he said. "I need a rest
If I'm to run and do my best."

Cow Dreams

What cow has not dreamed from afar
One day she'd be a moovie star,
To pose for klieg lights, make a name
In Hollywood and bask in fame,
Star in films, act, appear,
And build a pasteurized career,
Have an agent, dance and sing?
This would be the grandest thing,
Making slick "Got Milk?" commercials,
Fit these in between rehearsals,
Play the diva on the screen,
Razzle-dazzle, make the scene.
This a cow would love to do
If her wishes could come true.

Polar Bear's Complaints

Say, why is it, tell me,
I'm called a polar bear?
It's true that I am polar,
But bare is hard to bear.
With humans there must be
A whole lot of confusion
To say that I am bare
When in fact I'm usin'
Lots of fur to stay
Covered up and warm
Even in the midst
Of every winter storm.
Indeed, I always wear
My person in a coat
In all the arctic places
Northern and remote.
And please, won't you reveal—
Tell me what's the deal—
Why I've been called a thief
When it's only seals I steal?
Seal is what I eat,
And it's compulsory—
Thousands of them swimming
And living in the sea.
So knock it off, will ya?
Come on, folks, be nice,
'Cause don't you know my life
Is already on thin ice?

III. Animals Got Talent

Bears Jazzin'

On musical chairs a hip little band
Of magical bears sat jazzin' grand.

From forests, plains, hills up 'n' down
Critters came to hear their sound.

Razza-ma-tazz ... they played jazz!
Played it, baby ... Yazz, o' yazz!"

Joe on trumpet in bear fur coat
Blew every note clear outta his throat.

Razza-ma-tazz ... he played that jazz,
Did it like no bear ever has.

Hear what I'm sayin'? ... He was playin'
So sweet, even trees were swingin' and swayin'.

While Danny on drums went rum-a-tumm-tumm
With a rat-a-tat-tat and a pumm-ta-pumm-pumm.

Rat-a-tat-tat, he played like that;
Yes he did, he's one cool cat.

Play it bears! Play it loud!
Jazz the whole cool critter crowd.

Sam on sax jazzed to the max,
Sweet as sugar, smooth as fat.

And Sloan on trombone made it moan,
Played clear into the twilight zone.

"Waaah, waah, waah, raah, raah, raah
Slide it, Sloan-o, yaah, yaah, yaah!

Harlin on horn, made music bray
Smooth as silk, that-a-way.

Brass it, bear, toot for joy;
Play it like a big band toy.

Then there's Henry, don't forget,
Soloing on clarinet;

He's the one like no one yet
Playin' notes you'll not forget.

Groovy music made so thick
On his swaying licorice stick.

Fingers running, dashing 'round,
An amazing, phasing, crooning sound.

Play it, bears! All together,
Atmospherics like the weather.

Let it rain on every ear
Of every critter listening here.

Razza-ma-tazz ... Play that jazz!
Razza-ma-tazz ... Yazz o' yazz!

Razza-ma-tazz, this band of bears
Playing it here and everywhere.

Razza-ma-tazz, Razza-ma-tazz,
Play it bears like no one has!

Razza-ma-tazz, Razza-ma-tazz,
Keep it going ... Yazz o' yazz!

Elk and Welk

Have you heard of the amazing elk
Who sang and danced for Lawrence Welk?
He tried to make it on TV—
Move into the big leagues—but you see

The elk, though talented and appealing,
Soon encountered a high "glass ceiling,"
Which his antlers couldn't crash through,
No matter what he tried to do.

Thus this hoofing dancing elk,
Who auditioned not once, but twice for Welk,
Never made it to his stage,
Fell in a rut and then a rage.

But they gave him a consolation prize,
Which on the whole we think was wise.
Sometimes that's the way things go:
He couldn't buck the system but he made some dough.

Almost Famous

A tuna once claimed he began
His movie career when he swam
To France, rather far
To act and to star
Ending his career ... where? In Cannes!

After You

In Australia what would you do
Out golfing if a huge kangaroo
Came hopping your way?
Would you run or just say,
"Roo, after you, please play through!"

Giraffe Basketball

It has been said, there is a report,
That basketball is a giraffe's best sport—
Head and shoulders above all others
As every sports writer soon discovers.
Ask any lion or knowledgeable gnu
If it isn't so, if it isn't true,
And they will say without a quibble
Giraffes are famous for how they dribble
A basketball higher and farther than most,
Although they never brag or boast,
But simply do what giraffes do well.
Take one look and you can tell
This is their sport, and all in all
They do stand tall at basketball.

Winning Attitude

There was a fast rabbit named Jack,
A fellow who had a great knack
For winning each race,
Or at least he would place,
But, if not, he would vow to come back.

To Answer a Call

An amazing fellow, the octopus,
With eight arms ambidextrous.
If we give him a call,
He'll use arms, one and all,
To answer his cellphones and talk to us.

Birds Playing Musical Chairs

Like musical chairs from branch to branch,
Birds keep changing places;
Depending on their circumstance,
They navigate to new spaces
As if they're trying to decide
Where a better spot might be.
One by one each twig is tried,
A new perch found, from tree to tree.
It's almost like they play a game
Of moving, taking turns.
They land on branches not the same,
Yet each one onward yearns
To make a choice that proves the best
 Or better than the last to rest.

One Small Condition

We're The Monkeys—understand
We are a famous primate band
In the jungle where we sway;
Come and hear us play today!
Entertainment is our goal,
Why we swing with rock 'n' roll,
Sing with all our heart and soul,
Sometimes blues as well, a whole
Bunch of songs, while making plans
To perform and please our fans.
Won't you give our band a chance?
Come and see us, sing and dance.
But please know there's one condition:
Bring bananas for admission!

Piano Bird

Once I had a bird,
A bird that couldn't sing,
But this bird played piano—
Piano was its thing!

At first it played off key
And knew no harmony,
So practiced constantly
Underneath its tree!

Now you may think it odd
A bird could play at all,
Yet this one won applause
When it played Carnegie Hall!

Performing without music,
It winged it all the way,
Kept its place, didn't lose it,
Reviewers liked to say.

Indeed, it sold more tickets
Than most birds do today
That paid for seed and travel,
Which at first seemed A-okay.

But warning, people, warning!
I would not recommend
You get a bird like this one
To be your feathery friend.

Please listen, people, listen!
(Not to the bird, to me)
Because a bird like this one
Is not good company.

You could not stand its practice,
Or ever sit it out.
It practices all hours
Until you want to shout.

It's loud as loud can be,
And will not let you sleep
Due to its constant playing,
And occasional "Cheep! Cheep! Cheep!"

All this you can't endure
When quiet you'd prefer.
You'll grumble and you'll grrrr—
It's worse when you're on tour.

You'll wonder if it's worth it
To travel with this bird.
Flights aren't getting cheaper,
At least that's what I've heard.

It eats a lot of seed
And loudly munches crumbs.
The costs keep adding up
To astronomical sums.

No matter what the profits
This bird can generate,
If you score weekly concerts
They still aren't all that great.

So I warn you most sincerely,
And offer this advice:
Before you befriend a piano bird
Think long and hard, think twice,

Or I promise you'll be sorry
Because of what happened to me.
No matter the fame and glory
Your bird gains eventually,

It simply makes no sense
To feather your nest this way.
Don't give a bird a piano,
Or at least don't let it play!

IV. Small Tales

Papa Possum

Papa possum walks around
Thinking awesome thoughts profound,
Bound to educate his brood
When he finds they're in the mood
To hear his wise deliberations,
Perceptive truths he shares with patience,
Teaching things he knows make sense
Supported by good evidence.
Little possums are impressed
And will do their very best
To listen when he does instruct
How they should their lives conduct
In a way that's kind and true,
That is what smart possums do.

Wash for Dinner

A raccoon – this one was called Randy
At washing his food was quite handy.
He used his clawed paws
Cleaning food for his jaws
Since crawfish caught raw can be sandy.

Garter Snake Etiquette

When you see a small snake glide through grass
Don't bother it, know that it has
Places to go
In a hurry, not slow.
Stand back, step aside, let it pass.

Who You Resemble

High in a tree one dark night,
Except for the moon's reflected light,
A creature fierce, more vain than wise,
Asked a passing mouse, to its great surprise:

"Pray tell, little mouse, who do I resemble?
Tell me the truth and don't dissemble."
The mouse, with a quaver, scratched his head,
And thinking fast, here's what he said:

"Sir, you're not like a fox or hoppy hare,
You're not like a lynx, a wolf or a bear,
Certainly not like a bat or a deer,
Definitely not like those, I fear.

They're not at all who you resemble."
"Let me think a little more, so I don't dissemble,"
Squeaked the mouse, "Let's see, who do you resemble?
You're not like a badger, skunk or lark;

I could tell much easier if it weren't so dark.
You're definitely not like a bug eating bark.
None of these are who you resemble.
But to tell the truth, pardon if I tremble,

To say exactly who you resemble,
You definitely seem like someone bright
Especially here so near tonight,
And I just want to get it right

To describe who you're like, who you resemble.
I would say you resemble someone big,
Who could snap a neck like a little twig,
And while you're the finest fellow a mouse could know,

It's getting late and I really must go.
But as to who you really resemble,
Though I'd love to tell you and not dissemble,
Owl have to keep it a secret, friend,

For a time at least, till I don't know when.
Perhaps some night if we meet again,
Then I can tell you, and nicely, too,
Whoo you resemble, and tell you true.

I promise, friend, I really do,
I'll say then whooo you resemble."
At that the little mouse scampered along
Hoping and praying to be long gone

Before that monster had caught on
And one small mouse disassembled!
Yes, he skipped along, in fact, he ran,
Scurried, skedaddled, hurried, and

Hid as fast as a mouse can scram
Finding himself in such a jam.
And thus this tale ends happily:
The quick-witted mouse lived long and free.

As for the fellow perched in the tree,
He resembles himself, apparently.
But at night by the bright moonlight
He waits and watches and wonders, might

Having dinner been better than his vanity
And an empty stomach? (Most definitely!)

Mouse Repast

A mouse is a fellow mammal
Deserving our respect,
Like most with a hairy body,
Not least keen intellect.

We must admit it's clever
With instincts more than good,
An expert (Is it ever!)
When foraging for food.

It senses something tasty
By smell when food's around.
To a mouse it's buried treasure,
A pleasure to be found.

With that brief introduction,
Herein begins a tale
Of attempts we made to catch one
And our efforts to prevail.

It began with suspicious droppings
On our stove, two or three at most,
Followed by strange noises
That we joked must be a ghost.

Soon after that, however,
We saw a mouse, alright.
How agile and how quickly
It disappeared from sight!

We saw it in our kitchen;
Across our stove it ran.
We knew we had to catch it
And so we hatched a plan.

We did not wish to kill it,
So bought a humane trap
With a little door to enter,
But lacking an awful SNAP!

We placed the bait inside it
To draw the critter in
Down a narrow plastic hallway
Where its dinner could begin.

The bait was peanut butter,
A tempting tasty treat
Enticing to a mouse,
Who'd venture in to eat.

Like a little teeter-totter
The trap was built to tip;
The mouse's weight would trigger
The trap's small door to trip.

Inside the mouse'd be captured.
It could not turn and run,
Just eat the treat before it,
The bait it had, yum! Yum!

At least that was the theory
We decided we would test,
So set the trap and waited
Hoping for the best,

Then went about our business
Till later we heard a sound,
And sure enough inside the trap
A wee scared mouse we found!

The poor thing, how it trembled;
It had no place to hide.
We took it, trap and all,
A long, long way outside,

And there we set it free.
You should have seen it run.
So ended our adventure;
No harm to mouse was done.

The task we thought was over,
Our critter had been caught,
But just to be quite certain
Reset the trap in a different spot,

This time beneath our bathtub,
Snug, next to a pipe,
Then forgot it all day long
And went to bed that night.

In the morning when we checked it
We found something went wrong.
The trap door still was open
But inside the bait was gone!

How could this even happen?
Our failsafe trap had failed.
A mouse had gotten in and out
But never did get nailed!

So remember, mice are mammals
Deserving our respect.
Once fooled, they warn their pals
To outwit our intellect!

The Gray Squirrel

In the fall a squirrel goes nuts
Gathering his store,
Sensing winter's coming soon
As it has before.
Hiding nuts serves him well
Spreading out his larder.
When he tries to dig nuts up,
That can prove far harder.
Is one here? Where, oh where?
Is one over there?
A squirrel must wonder, really ponder,
When his cupboard's bare.
A squirrel goes digging, digging, digging,
Hunting for his treasure,
Hoping smell and memory
Will bring him food and pleasure.
Searching nuts, that is what
A squirrel is wont to do —
Find 'em, dig 'em, brush 'em off,
Crack their shells and chew!
The squirrel goes leaping, leaping, leaping,
Acrobating, sometimes creeping,
Till the snow of winter heaping
Finds him nestled, safely sleeping,
Dozing deeply, sleeping fast,
Till the winter's worst is past.
What we call his hibernation
To the squirrel is like vacation.

The Skunk

Skunk scent is a sort of blessing
Reminding us not to be messing
With his kind or else you
May encounter his pee-yoo!

A skunk—that is, the common type—
Is black with one back narrow stripe
Down the center and it's white,
Bright enough to see at night.

His tail looks like a little bush
Which he wears above his tush,
And nearby he has a gland
That makes a smell no one can stand.

If you corner him, he may
Quickly spray and run away
Leaving a stench that people say
Will make you stink and reek all day.

Then you'll want a deep bathtub
To bathe in, wash in, scrub-a-dub,
After which you'll burn your clothes,
And besides those shoes dispose.

The smell of skunks is more than bad,
And you'll know it if you've had
A run-in with one, chanced to meet,
With your car out on a street.

It is sad though, sad to say
So many die this way today
Crossing, as skunks often may
A busy road or broad highway.

From a skunk's own point of view
This is truly tragic, too,
Since all he wants to do is roam
Without car troubles near his home.

The Beetle and the Horseshoe

*When they came to shoe the horses,
the beetle stretched out his leg.
—English Proverb*

When they came to shoe the horse,
A beetle stretched out his leg.
"I'm first," he said importantly.
(He'd take the horse down a peg.)

"My feet are far more worthy here
For shoeing than yours, horse.
Move aside," the beetle cried,
"Lest I resort to force."

The horse, of course, thought this absurd
And whinnied in reply,
"Why, you are just a tiny bug
No bigger than a fly.

"You're so small, hardly there at all!
Were I to take a step
I'd flatten you with my horseshoe.
It'd crush you, you can bet.

"You're way too proud, and talking loud
Does not favorably impress.
You act like you are mighty big,
While I see you are far less.

"And here you come into this stall
For service right away.
You must think you are awfully fine
To strut and act this way."

The beetle gasped, was really shocked
To be talked to in that way.
Horse hadn't heard the end of this,
No sir, no how, no way!

"Out of my way!" the beetle cried,
As he approached with pride and pomp.
"Step aside and let me pass."
That's when the horse went STOMP!

The Hedgehog

The hedgehog is no hog at all;
When threatened rolls into a ball.
It's short and small, not large or tall,
With high-pitched voice to squeak its call.

In forests far away it dwells,
And green grasslands or deep dells
Are places where it hides to thrive
Undisturbed, to stay alive.

If you've not met a hedgehog, know
It moves around, though rather slow.
Nocturnal, an insectivore,
It has both spines and hair galore.

In short, the hedgehog is an animal
Much like us, a type of mammal,
Except, of course, we don't have spines
Or resemble its kin, the porcupine.

But as distant cousins, we're related,
Strange as it seems, in nature created.
We walk on two legs, hedgehogs four;
They hug the ground while humans soar.

There's more to tell about this critter,
Facts to mention and consider,
Some impressive, this is true;
I'd check them out if I were you.

V. Four-legged Tales

Fox with Moxie

The fox is full of moxie,
Shrewd as any dude.
Thus we say he's foxy
And it's understood
What we mean is clever,
Wily in his ways,
Cunning; is he ever
Canny, and displays
Traits that keep him living,
Not an easy thing—
Surviving, even thriving,
Raising new offspring.
He might not seem about,
Yet likely is around.
Quiet as all get-out,
He rarely makes a sound.
This is just his habit,
Hunting day-to-day
To catch a careless rabbit
Or rodent, as he may.
If by luck or happenstance
You spot him, know it's rare
To even catch the briefest glance
Before he isn't there.
Then he's gone just like a ghost,
A moment's fascination.
Was he real or at the most
Your wild imagination?

One Sly Fox

One sly fox,
Is he clever?
Fools the hounds,
Hides in heather.
Crosses stream,
Gets away.
Is he smart?
I should say!

Acacia Devotee

A giraffe is a very tall beast.
If you wonder on what it will feast,
It's acacia tree leaves,
Every one it can seize,
With its neck fifteen feet at the least.

Elephant Walk

"Pack your trunk," said the elephant
To her child. "We must move out.
It's time you learned, my baby dear,
What our wide world is about.

"We must walk north across the veldt;
The land here is too dry.
Up north there's greener grass to eat;
It's sweet, in good supply.

"Come, follow me, my little one.
Stay close; I'll show the way.
We need to leave—I mean right now—
And start without delay."

And so the mama pachyderm
Packed up, and with her son
Began to trod across the veldt
Avoiding midday sun.

Hyenas followed, jackals too,
The way they always do,
While from a distance lions watched
Who also could pursue.

Day and night, night and day,
They traveled on past dark,
Munching grass not dried or brown
And their favorite food, tree bark.

They dug deep holes in dry creek beds
To find springs underground,
Dipped their trunks to drink their fill,
Glad for what they found.

Other herds were going, too,
Across the endless plain.
Another season they'd return
When thunder came and rain.

Mile after mile, day after day,
They trudged and sometimes ran
Alongside wary wildebeest
Now fewer than began.

Vultures circled overhead
And watched for weak to die.
The fittest of the herd moved on
Below where lions lie.

"Stay close. Don't stray, my little one.
You're safe if you keep near."
So spoke the mama elephant,
And nudged her baby dear.

On they went with patient gait.
Each day they stopped for water,
What little they could find,
To drink what rivers brought there.

"Keep up, my dear. Don't lag behind.
You must not walk so slow.
Beyond the far horizon, son,
Is where sweet grasses grow."

"I'm tired, mama, tuckered out.
Please tell me, is it far,
A mile or more, where we must walk
To find where grasses are?"

"Not terribly far, my baby dear,"
His mama made reply.
"We'll make it if we just keep on;
You'll make it if you try."

Her baby's legs were short; his steps
Not half as long as hers.
Although he struggled to keep up,
His progress had grown worse.

A lion in the distance saw
Him stumble. What was this?
A weakened baby elephant?
A straggler not to miss?

The lion's pride, the watchful cats,
Prepared to make a kill.
They moved in slowly, quietly;
That night they'd eat their fill.

The mama elephant saw the cats
And felt a frightful chill.
Determined to protect her son,
She summoned up her will.

Closer in the lions crept,
Half hidden, from all sides,
Though grass that's dry and eaten down
Or trampled poorly hides.

The mama urged her son along;
Nudging him to run.
Her sisters guessed as well as she
From where the charge would come.

The lions readied for their move;
Then several stopped, gave pause.
One angry mother elephant
Might crush their careless claws,

But with her sisters gathered round,
Her baby to defend,
The lions faced a great gray wall—
They'd better think again.

And so they left to take a nap;
They'd find far easier prey.
Their stomachs still were mostly full
From a kill just yesterday.

Another day, not as hard,
Of travel passed and then
The elephants found greener grass,
All safe at journey's end.

Moral: Stay close, keep up, protect your own,
And nurture nature's ties;
Therein lies strength, and so at length
Who does this well survives.

A Bear and Bees

The hum of bees from honey trees
Attracts a bear exactly where
Their golden sweets provide good eats.
The burly bear, though half aware
The bees are there, just doesn't care
The bees intend their sweets to spare.
He wants to fetch himself a treat,
And will not let the bees defeat
His feasting till it is complete.
Indeed, as far as he's concerned
His efforts bring a treat much earned,
So stings of bees will just be spurned
Till he completes his honey forage
To sweeten up his morning porridge.

The Graceful Giraffe

The giraffe with slender neck so long
Is graceful, gainly, tall beyond
Other creatures in its height
In Africa, a marvelous sight,
A tower of power with overview,
Camouflaged neck and nimble, too,
A work of nature gloriously,
An acacias-feeder, carefully.
This he is, a desert star,
Above most animals by far,
A work of art, a masterpiece,
Second to none, a stunning beast,
From ground up and without a flaw,
A creature worthy of our awe.

A Simple Life

Want to be happy? Here is how:
Live life like your average cow
Who stays at ease, free from care,
Walks in her pasture, breathes fresh air.
Ways of the world are no concern;
She need not hustle nor a living earn.
She's content, provided for,
Neither rich nor ever poor.
It's true at times she may feel bossy,
Somewhat moo-dy, a bit saucy,
Yet without angst, no sad "Alas!"
Just eats her grass and let's gas pass,
Happily grazing with her herd—
To do otherwise has not occurred.

The Savanna Elephant

The savanna elephant weighs four tons
Counting belly, trunk, tusks, and buns,
And surprisingly it runs quite fast
When charging with its mighty mass.

Its ears are rather strange to see;
They work like fans, cool as can be.
Its trunk, of course, has a clever twist
To pick up food much like a fist.

And as for its more than modest tail,
Good reasons for it simply fail;
It's dull gray skin might not impress us,
Though a leathery hide can weather stresses.

With legs like posts and great flat feet,
It trods the ground to drink and eat.
It's said the beast may not see well,
But compensates with keenest smell.

All in all, a noble creature,
To its young a gentle teacher,
Loyal to its family, yet
With a mind that won't forget;

For once well met, it will remember
Who you are January to December.
Though huge, it's humble, means no harm,
And displays an elephantastic charm.

Be kind to the elephant—let it roam
Across the veldt, its savanna home.

The White-tailed Deer

How charming, gentle, shy, demure
We find a doe, a white-tailed deer,
Nearby with her sleepy fawn
One misty morning just at dawn.
We watch them from our forest lodge,
Fawn in dappled camouflage,
Both alert, ready to run
If a predator should come.
Then off they bound in a flash,
Long legs moving with a dash.
Animated by their fear,
Just like ghosts they disappear,
Vanished so quickly it can seem
As if they were only a dream.

VI. To Sea What We Can See

The Starfish

On a sandy bar from foamy sea
A starfish washed ashore to me.
Its being there was simple chance,
Yet one I noticed with a glance.
What have we here, I said to me,
With five short legs and skin bumpy?
What creature here has sought me out?
(Asked I, though this was not in doubt.)
Then lifting it up from the sand
I found it barely filled my hand,
A natural wonder resting there
And most likely well aware
That such as me it did not know,
And so I let the creature go.

The Seahorse

The seahorse is no horse at all;
It's way too tiny, far too small.
It will not whinny should you call,
Or even jump a paddock wall.

It only swims deep in the sea;
A true horse therefore cannot be.
It does not gallop, will not trot,
And weighs just ounces, not a lot.

Unlike most fish, it's rarely caught,
Although in pet stores some are bought.
A true horse may let people ride,
But this one swims below the tide.

So as you see, the seahorse can't
Be a true horse, no, and shan't.
You cannot saddle up this one,
Nor ride it toward the setting sun.

So how then did it get its name?
It has its lovely shape to blame—
Resembling the head of any horse,
Which led to naming it, of course.

Go to a large aquarium
And likely you can see it swim,
Hovering among seaweed,
This charming swimming horse-like steed.

Piranha Lunch

"I'm terribly hungry," said a young piranha.
"Let's do lunch. Anyone wanna?"
"Sounds good to us," his school friends said.
"Swim on, buddy! Let's get fed."

Oh, the Amazon flows, it's a mighty river,
Taker of life or generous giver.
To some it's lunch around the bend,
To others it's where they meet their end.

It wasn't long till that hungry band
Of piranha thought they smelled a hand.
Dip-dip-dipping beside a canoe,
Breakin' water as it paddled through.

"Hand ahoy!" cried the young piranha.
"Finger food is what we wanna
Chew right here to make our lunch.
Come on, gang. Let's munch, munch, munch!"

Oh, the Amazon flows, it's a mighty river,
Taker of life or generous giver.
To some it's lunch around the bend,
To others it's where they meet their end.

Under the canoe came bubble, bubble!
Look out fingers! Trouble! Trouble!
Look out hand and look out wrist!
Piranha attack! Or had they missed?

Aboard the canoe there arose a roar,
Men all shouting, "Head for shore!
Watch your fingers, paddle faster.
Quick! Or face piranha disaster!"

Oh, the Amazon flows, it's a mighty river,
Taker of life or generous giver.
To some it's lunch around the bend,
To others it's where they meet their end.

The sleek canoe soon reached the shore;
Finger food was there no more.
It was bye-bye-bye to lunch, delicious,
Tough luck, piranha, starved and vicious!

School dismissed, food all gone,
But another chance would come along.
Piranhas this time missed a bite,
But next time they might get it right.

Oh, the Amazon flows, it's a mighty river,
Taker of life or generous giver.
To some it's lunch around the bend,
To others it's where they meet their end.

Some days are lucky, some are not,
But listen up, tell you what:
Paddle the Amazon how you may,
But keep piranha fish at bay
And keep your fingers far away!

No Boat for Crocodile Throat

By the Nile a crocodile
Lies and suns himself in style
Waiting, watching all the while
For a meal to make him smile.
When a small boat glides his way,
The crocodile calls it play

To knock it over; a buffet
Awaits him and may make his day.
Say, crocodile, by the Nile,
Keep on sleeping, stay awhile.
Do not, do not start to swim
To the boat I'm riding in.

Find some better thing to do
Than bite my little boat in two,
Crocodile, in your style,
Lying by the muddy Nile.
I'm watching, have my eyes on you,
So keep your distance, see you do.

Crocodile with guile, deceit,
I'm not the meal you're going to eat.
Let me pass by, paddle, float;
This time you can miss the boat.
Know my flesh has less appeal
Than others who could make your meal.

Goodbye, sunning crocodile,
Monster of the lower Nile.
I'm leaving now, I'm on my way.
Fare thee well, goodbye, good day!

Blue Marlins

Why is it marlins seem so blue?
What can we this attribute to?
Is it because they're out to sea
But do not really wish to be?

That the way they live is fathoms deep
And have a hard time getting sleep?
Or can't get good psychiatry?
Can't get insurance to pay the fee?

We could say: "Get in the swim,
Exercise more, get back your vim,
Avoid what's nettlesome—the very thing
That any fishing boat might bring.

 "Dwell not on your deficiencies,
Meditate more, try to be
Not hooked on scams and never bite
On lures or bait or be up-tight.

"Never get your heads above water
Like one did and then someone caught her.
Don't equate your gills with guilt
Nor swim near river mouths with silt.

"So listen up, marlins, 'cause if you do
These things will likely see you through;
An ocean of fun will open for you
And no matter your color you won't be blue."

Wonders of the Octopus

The wonders of the octopus
Are more than merely marvelous.
Intelligent, though rather shy,
Its IQ we can see is high
And has to be with arms, all eight,
It must control, coordinate,
With hearts that beat, not one but three,
Together most amazingly.
But when it sees a need to flee
It will retreat most rapidly,
Change color fast and in a blink
Disappear in clouds of ink.
So we see upon inspection
Invisibility is its best protection.

Meditation on Returning Salmon

Here today,
Spawn tomorrow!

Catch a Bite to Eat

A grizzly bear appears quite bright
When catching salmon, his delight.
He waits where they leap
For the bounty he'll reap,
And grabs them in flight with one bite.

VII. Feathered Tales

Peacock Eyes

How many eyes has a peacock?
Depends on how you count.
Some say two, others deadlock
Disputing the amount.
Should we include the feather eyes
Plus peepers on its head?
The numbers combined may surprise:
Two dozen it's been said.
But is that right? Is it true?
Who has ever counted, you?
In a book? Or at the zoo?
On male birds or on females, too?
When one wanders down your path,
I advise you do the math!

Penguin Parade

Penguins led a great parade
Across bright slippery ice.
Each one brave, none afraid;
All were tough and wise.
Said one, "No need for us to hurry
For we are doing fine.
There is no point to rush or scurry,
Let's all just stay in line.
Straight on is good, well understood;
It is the shortest way
To reach the shore, catch fish galore,
To rest and nest and play.
Besides, the ice is dangerous,
A detour would seem strange to us."

The Bird Nest

A bird on a branch built a nest
With artistry she did her best
Until a strong breeze
Blew hard through the trees,
And gave her good work a strong test.

So did her small nest, her sweet home,
Survive the stiff breeze, hold its own,
Built well out of sticks
To harbor her chicks?
The answer might still be unknown.

But if we would hazard a guess
About failure, or better, success,
Chances are good
The nest has withstood
That breeze, so the answer is yes!

And sure enough, later that fall
When the nest was found fallen, a ball,
In form it was sound
Intact on the ground!
It had done its job well after all.

Owl Scowl

A lark spied a great owl
Who gave her quite a scowl.
The lark looked far away,
Decided not to stay.
Said owl, "Lark, wait there, dear.
Fear not, you mustn't fly."
The lark thought owl too near,
Thought best to say goodbye.
And so away lark went;
The owl watched with dismay.
Its threat seemed evident,
What more was there to say?
When owl scowls at a lark,
'Tis best she flee the park!

A Vee of Geese

A vee of geese flies from the east
To land upon a pond,
Circles round and then is pleased
To rest before going on.
It's fun to watch these big birds land,
And ease into the water,
A marvel and a feat that's grand;
One wonders how they got here.
It must have taken weeks of straining
To reach here from afar.
Where did they gain their aerial training
To navigate by a star?
It must be such a natural gift
That comes with wings that flap and lift.

Feeding Cranes

The sun was young, the day was, too.
The sky rose rose, then turned light blue.
Birds woke early, wide awake;
Fish were jumping in the lake.
The wind was pushing waves about,
When on the shore two cranes came out,
Breakfast on their minds to seek
Discriminating with each beak,
Picking here, poking there,
Watching with a thoughtful stare,
For what foods were tasty, close,
Careful in the ones they chose,
Mindful with their frequent picks
Of what would nourish waiting chicks.

Turkey Survival

How is it that some turkeys thrive,
Even manage to stay alive?
I have wondered, as might you,
Speculating how they do.
It's true smart turkeys know to run
Away from danger and have fun,
Although Thanksgiving can be tough
For many, even more than rough.
But if they skip this holiday,
Keep on living day-to-day,
And can use good feather sense
When their captors plan events,
Then some turkeys need not worry
If they do their hiding early.

Royal Peacocks

Peacocks with a hundred eyes
And feathered fan, these we prize;
How they stand proud together
Iridescent every feather!
When did they become so bright,
Almost glowing in the light,
Each with built-in royal throne
Common birds would love to own?
Heads held up, necks smoothed down,
Decorated with a crown,
Our attention to command,
Showing us they're more than grand
In their kingdom when they pause,
Implying they expect applause.

Four Foolish Crows

Four crows in a row argued where to go.
Said the first, "Let's fly to Mexico,
For there the air is warm and sweet
And full of bugs, all we can eat."

The second blinked and scratched his head.
"I have a far better idea," he said.
"Instead of south, fly north, I say;
It's a mosquito paradise there every day."

"Wait!" cried the third. "I'll have you know
East is the place we ought to go,
Where wiggly worms would have us come
To eat them up—yum! Yum! Yum! Yum!"

"Birds!" cried the fourth. "Crow-operate!
It's already fall. It's getting late.
Let's all agree we should head west.
West, I say, west is best."

"Hold your feathers," cawed an older crow,
Listening on a branch below.
"Before you head in any direction,
Let me ask one simple question:

"Why does it matter which way you choose?
If you pick just one, three others you lose.
And if it proves no better than three,
Why waste your time to disagree?"

The four crows paused—his advice made sense.
They began to relax—no need to be tense.
Whichever way picked was good as another;
No need to bicker, brother-to-brother.

So one flew north and one flew south;
One flew east; another west.
Why disagree? Why chitter-chatter,
When it really didn't matter?

What really mattered was getting along,
In harmony to sing birdsong.
What mattered most was staying friends.
And on that note our story ends.

VIII. What's in a Name?

A Gnu Spelling

It's news to gnus (and who's to blame?)
That gnus have a "g" to start their name.
This spelling's lame, but all the same
Perhaps the "g" adds to gnus' fame,

Gives them class and more attention
By this inventive, odd convention.
Though one must ask, or at least mention,
Why was this done? What strange intention

Caused such spelling with a "g"?
What explanation can there be?
Does this make sense to me or you
To use a "g" to spell a gnu?

Not to me. What do you say
About the spelling done this way?
I say we drop the "g" on gnu
And end it with an "e," that, too.

N—U—E makes sense to me;
Let's change "gnu" if we both agree,
And do what sensible folks would do:
Out with the old, in with the nue.

The Zonkey

The zonkey exists—not kidding you—
Roams free in Kenya with a few at the zoo.
A zebra and donkey mated together
To produce this result, rather clever.
Instead of stripes, its skin has spots,
Or if you prefer call them dots,
Black coloration on a field of white;
This is the truth—you've read it right.
It's strong, not too stubborn, as far as we know,
There are only a few, which may stay so.
Search on its name and you will see
It actually exists, incredibly.
Go ahead and have a stare.
This animal is rather rare.*

----
*The zonkey is about as rare as the zony and
the zorse, while donkras and hebras are even rarer!

The Peliphant

A peliphant can be elegant
When found in combination
As a pelican and elephant
In our imagination.

One brings a bill, the other trunk,
And when they mix the two,
We have to say we'd never thunk
About all these two could do.

We knew they wouldn't fly as well
As the elephant half might wish
By flapping ears, and who can tell
Whether it would eat fish,

Not be repelled by a fishy smell,
Though its pelican part could eat
Any fish found in its bill,
A connoisseur bird's treat.

But as to flying part elephant,
Know it couldn't go by plane
Or pack its trunk with clothes and junk
Or a boarding pass obtain.

Though a pelican would gladly try
To do this, and to learn
The tricks of travel; it could fly,
Unlike a pachyderm.

Yet remember that an elephant
Remembers, and it must,
How to survive, and let's be blunt,
Argue points with both its tusks,

And could adapt if its ears would flap,
Open to a new endeavor,
While a pelican can't bridge the gap
To change—it's not that clever.

However, when the two do mate
And work well as a team,
They've many powers unknown to date,
At least so it would seem.

For the peliphant, half elephant,
Part pelican the other half,
Deserves respect, which we should grant,
Let's be serious, folks, don't laugh.

The Leopon

Once I met a leopon,
A hybrid at the zoo,
A leopard/lion mix
In India – it's true!
His coat has lots of spots
With regal mane on top,
The mane is from his mom
The pattern's from his pop.
Fierce as a cat can be,
He's two in one, you see.

Mongooses

"Mongooses," there's a word for you,
It's plural, as you see,
Not spelled "mongeese," when three or two,
Most linguists will agree.
Yet "goose" is "goose" and "geese" are "geese";
With birds we say it's so.
Again convention this decrees
As most of us well know.
Consistency, quite honestly,
In English won't apply.
Thus "mongeese" is quite definitely
Wrong—please don't ask me why.
We simply use it as we do.
Does that sound reasonable to you?

Defamed Misnamed Animals

Have you ever noticed that the skunk
Has a name that rhymes (past tense) with "stunk"?
And that his cousin, the lovely mink,
Evokes (present tense) a word like "stink"?

Not to mention the weasel and the duck,
Combined with "out" are out of luck!
And Wisconsin's badger, let's state here,
Suffers from "bad" in its nomenclature?

Recall as well the fox of fable
Is slandered as sly, likewise the sable.
Then who can fault a sensitive critter
So defamed from feeling bitter?

In truth, we humans have no shame
When it comes to labeling. We're to blame.
Through stereotypes and other slights
We've tagged such animals in the worst of lights.

We sully them and their reputations,
Besmirch their characters with word associations,
And doing so show no regret.
But just you wait, because I'll bet

Creatures big and creatures small,
Every critter short or tall,
Will band together, their goal the same:
To demand we give them a better name.

The skunk and mink will have their say.
They can hardly wait for that reckoning day.
Until no "stink" will embarrass the mink,
No "skunk" again will rhyme with "stunk."

They'll ferret us out in a pig-headed way
To get our goat, dog us, not only horseplay.
They'll pay us back, if not just yet,
In ways we will not soon forget.

"What's in a name?" is no small matter
For animals names are more than patter.
Someday, we predict, animals will rejoice
When they rise and demand names of their choice!

The X-itee

Exotic is the x-itee,
A creature of complexity.
Indeed, it is a rarity
Found only in a distant sea,

And even there, peculiarly,
Not with any certainty
Because it's small, apparently,
In fact so microscopically

Some argue, and convincingly,
It might not be there actually
Since no one's ever seen the beast
North or south, west or east,

At least not very frequently,
Which makes it more reliably
A beast of fiction we will see
Only in rhymed poetry,

And there so seldom, even yet,
Or in an animal alphabet!

The Frumious Bandersnatch

It's hard to see, much less to catch,
The elusive frumious Bandersnatch.
We've often tried and done our best,
But always failed to pass the test.
When we went to, it went fro;
When we moved fast, it went slow;
Around and 'round we'd somehow go,
It way up high, us down below.
We never ever seemed to match,
Us and the frumious Bandersnatch.
Though naturally we tried to see
Where we thought it ought to be.
Though many a plan we tried to hatch,
We never could catch the Bandersnatch.

The Unicorn You May See

A unicorn is a horse with a horn
That grows from the day it is born.
With this borne in mind
You will most often find
He travels out early each morn.

But pretend you don't see him there so
He will stay where he is and not go,
For to see such a sight
Is a magic delight
When he prances and preens, as you know.

He does this a lot, for you see
It makes him feel cute and carefree.
Other places to look
To find him are a book
Or perhaps on a bright tapestry.

That's when he's viewed at his best,
Full of vinegar, vigor, and zest;
Then and forthwith
He can transcend his myth
Or so he will often attest.

If you don't believe this is so
And you've searched for the truth high and low,
Then we recommend
That you and a friend
Visit your library where they will know.

What Birds Are

Say which it is
That birds are:
Angels of bliss
Or dinosaur?
Observe the facts
Of DNA,
Look at their tracks,
Let fancy play.
It's yours to choose
Which way to go,
Win or lose,
Who's to know?
Call a bird a heavenly star
Or settle for a dinosaur.

About the Author

Jeffry Glover, winner of a Robert Frost Foundation poetry award and a top ten Outstanding Leader in Education award, creates delightful rhyming poems and tales in verse. He draws upon his experience as a school librarian, language arts teacher, book editor, and library games inventor to produce collections of verse that are in turn whimsical and witty, humorous and heartwarming, serious, and just plain fun to read. As a library promotion specialist, his work has reached millions of children and adults around the world to encourage reading and exploring libraries. In retirement Jeff is publishing multiple volumes of poetry collected over his many years of writing. He is the author of over 7,000 sonnets on almost every topic under the sun. Visit Jeffry's website at PoetryPie.com or scan the QR code to check out more of Jeff's books, poetry videos, and sampler poems at PoemsforPleasurePress.com!

www.ingramcontent.com/pod-product-compliance
Lightning Source LLC
Chambersburg PA
CBHW030155100526
44592CB00009B/296